BEARCUB BIOS

LIN-MANUEL MIRANDA

COMPOSER, SINGER, AND ACTOR

by Rachel Rose

Consultant: Beth Gambro
Reading Specialist, Yorkville, Illinois

BEARPORT
PUBLISHING

Minneapolis, Minnesota

Teaching Tips

BEFORE READING

- Look at the cover of the book. Discuss the picture and the title.

- Ask readers to brainstorm a list of what they already know about Lin-Manuel Miranda, including what they learned from the cover. What can they expect to see in this book?

- Go on a picture walk, looking through the pictures to discuss vocabulary and make predictions about the text.

DURING READING

- Read for purpose. Encourage readers to look for key pieces of information they can expect to see in biographies.

- Ask readers to look for the details of the book. What happened to Lin-Manuel Miranda at different times of his life?

- If readers encounter an unknown word, ask them to look at the sounds in the word. Then, ask them to look at the rest of the page. Are there any clues to help them understand?

AFTER READING

- Encourage readers to pick a buddy and reread the book together.

- Ask readers to name three things Lin-Manuel Miranda has done throughout his life. Go back and find the pages that tell about these things.

- Ask readers to write or draw something they learned about Lin-Manuel Miranda.

Credits:
Cover and title page ©Tinseltown/Shutterstock and ©Titikul_B/Shutterstock, 3, ©John Shearer/Getty Images; 5, ©Walter McBride/Getty Images; 7, ©Walter McBride/Getty Images; 8, ©Gerard SIOEN/Getty Images; 11, ©Andrew H. Walker/Getty Images; 13, ©Bruce Glikas/Getty Images; 14, ©Alberto E. Rodriguez/Getty Images; 16, ©Alberto E. Rodriguez/Getty Images; 19, ©Gladys Vegas/Getty Images; 21, ©Bruce Glikas/Getty Images; 22, ©Roy Rochlin/Getty Images; 23, ©Paul Morigi/Getty Images; 23, ©Adel Newman/Shutterstock; 23, ©Rido/Shutterstock

Library of Congress Cataloging-in-Publication Data

Names: Rose, Rachel, 1968- author.
Title: Lin-Manuel Miranda : composer, singer, and actor / Rachel Rose.
Description: Minneapolis : Bearport Publishing Company, 2021. | Series: Bearcub bios | Includes bibliographical references and index.
Identifiers: LCCN 2020054967 (print) | LCCN 2020054968 (ebook) | ISBN 9781647478438 (library binding) | ISBN 9781647478513 (paperback) | ISBN 9781647478599 (ebook)
Subjects: LCSH: Miranda, Lin-Manuel, 1980---Juvenile literature. | Composers--United States--Biography--Juvenile literature. | Lyricists--United States--Biography--Juvenile literature. | Actors--United States--Biography--Juvenile literature.
Classification: LCC ML3930.M644 R67 2021 (print) | LCC ML3930.M644 (ebook) | DDC 782.1/4092 [B]--dc23
LC record available at https://lccn.loc.gov/2020054967
LC ebook record available at https://lccn.loc.gov/2020054968

For more information, write to Bearport Publishing, 5357 Penn Avenue South, Minneapolis, MN 55419. Printed in the United States of America.

Contents

It's a Hit!

Lin-Manuel Miranda was very happy.

His **musical** *Hamilton* was a big hit.

He wrote the show.

He acted and sang in it, too!

Lin-Manuel's Life

Lin-Manuel was born in New York.

His parents are from an **island** called Puerto Rico.

Growing up, Lin-Manuel spent many summers there.

Lin-Manuel's mother

Lin-Manuel's father

8

Lin-Manuel always loved music.

He saw his first musical when he was seven.

Soon, he sang and acted in shows, too.

When he was 19, Lin-Manuel started writing a musical.

It took him years to finish it.

The show was called *In the Heights*.

People loved it!

Then, Lin-Manuel worked on other musicals.

He wrote *Hamilton*.

It was about early U.S. history.

The show had **hip-hop** music.

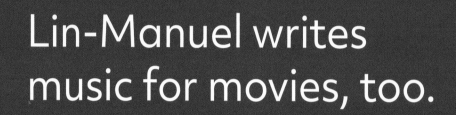

Lin-Manuel writes music for movies, too.

He made songs for the Disney movie *Moana*.

He has loved Disney since he was a kid.

15

Lin-Manuel also acts in TV shows and movies.

In 2018, he was in *Mary Poppins Returns*.

He played the part of Jack.

Lin-Manuel finds time to help people.

There was a very bad storm in Puerto Rico.

Lin-Manuel went to the island to help.

Lin-Manuel is a star.

He writes music and hit shows.

He sings and acts.

And he wants to do even more!

21

Did You Know?

Born: January 16, 1980

Family: Luz (mother), Luis (father), Luz (sister)

When he was a kid: He played the piano. His father says he was not very good!

Special fact: Growing up, Lin-Manuel spoke Spanish with his family.

Lin-Manuel says: "Fill the world with music, love, and **pride**."

Life Connections

Lin-Manuel found what he loved to do when he was young. And he kept doing it. What do you love to do? Do you think you could do it forever?

Glossary

hip-hop a kind of rap music

island land with water on all sides

musical a show that tells a story with music

pride a feeling that you are important

Index

Read More

Calkhoven, Laurie. *Lin–Manuel Miranda (You Should Meet)*. New York: Simon Spotlight, 2018.

Friesen, Helen Lepp. *Puerto Rico (Explore the U.S.A.)*. New York: AV2 by Weigl, 2019.

Learn More Online

1. Go to **www.factsurfer.com**
2. Enter "**Lin-Manuel Miranda**" into the search box.
3. Click on the cover of this book to see a list of websites.

About the Author

Rachel Rose is a writer who lives in San Francisco. Her favorite books to write are those about people who lead inspiring lives.